Weird, Wacky, and Unexpected Moments in Sports

SPORTS BLOOPERS

Phyllis and Zander Hollander

Illustrated with photographs

An Associated Features Book

SCHOLASTIC INC.
New York Toronto London Auckland Sydney

ISBN 0-590-43712-7

Copyright © 1985 by Associated Features, Inc. All rights reserved. Published by Scholastic Inc.

12 11 10 9 8

789/9

Printed in the U.S.A.

23

CONTENTS

Introduction 5

A Catcher's Lot Is Not
a Happy One 6

Mix-up at the Plate 6

Branca's Burden 7

Hat Stuff 8

Wrong-Way Riegels 10

Spin Series 11

Tackle from the Bench 12

Forced Landing 13

Touchdown 13

A Shattering Experience 14

Brief Encounter 15

The Official Ball 15

Bursting the Bubble 16

A Perfect Strike 17

Fun and Games 18

Illegal Assist 20

Fallen Hopes 21

On the Way to Greatness 22

The Long Count 24

Splashdown 25

Dinner on Ice 26

"Slap Shot" 27

Oops! 28

Sternoisms 29

The Superstars 30

Mile-a-Minute Murphy 32

Mud Battle 33

The Babe Strikes Out 34

The Other Babe 35

Presidents at Play 36

Historic Mask 38

Faceless Pirate 39

Bird Fever 40

Phillie Phanatic 41

Side Show 42

Look Out Below! 44

High Kick 45

"Yer Out!" 45

The Stormy World of
Mighty Mac 46

Battle of the Sexes 48

No Comic on the
Playing Field 49

Good Morning, David 50

Yogi to the Fore 51

Packey East 52

Surprise for the Champ 53

"The Rifleman" 54

"The Natural" 56

The Sporting Matthau 57

On the Way to the
White House 58

A Saturday Hero 59

Garden Variety 60

Gnats to You 62

Roll Out the Barrel 63

Circling the Globetrotters 64

INTRODUCTION

You are about to enter the world of the unexpected in sports. You will get to meet the player who ran the wrong way in the Rose Bowl; the catcher who blew it when he missed a vital third strike in the World Series; the pitcher most famous for having given up a home run in a National League playoff; the fullback who came off the bench as a twelfth man to tackle a ball-carrier in the Cotton Bowl; the figure skater who fell and lost a chance at an expected gold medal; a Minnesota Viking fan who piloted his hot-air balloon into the stands at the Super Bowl; an Olympic marathon runner who was helped across the finish line by the officials.

You will see pitcher Tom Seaver catching a pie in his face; quarterback Joe Theismann bowling; outfielder Reggie Jackson weightlifting; Darryl Dawkins shattering a backboard; third baseman George Brett in a bubble gum contest; President John F. Kennedy, Cassius Clay (Muhammad Ali), Pete Rose, and Chuck Connors as kids.

You'll come across Billie Jean King defeating Bobby Riggs in tennis' "Battle of the Sexes"; *Good Morning, America*'s David Hartman hitting in spring training with the Dodgers; Tug McGraw riding Phillie Phanatic; Bob Hope boxing; President Ronald Reagan starring as a football player; Robert Redford batting for the New York Knights.

Assembled here in a circus of sports, they make up an all-star cast of athletes, actors, comedians, Presidents, and radio and TV announcers who were caught by the camera at just the right moment.

Phyllis and Zander Hollander

A Catcher's Lot Is Not a Happy One

It happened in the 1941 World Series. The New York Yankees had won two of the first three games against the Brooklyn Dodgers. And now the Dodgers, playing at home at Ebbets Field, were leading, 4–3, bottom of the ninth, in the fourth game. Brooklyn relief pitcher Hugh Casey retired the first two batters, then got two strikes on Tommy Henrich. Casey threw a fast curve, Henrich missed it and so did catcher Mickey Owen, who chased the ball to the backstop as Henrich reached first safely. The Yankees then put together a single, double, walk, another double and suddenly they had a 7–4 victory. The next day the Yankees won, 3–1, to capture the World Series. "It was all my fault," said Owen, the catcher who lost the curve ball. Nobody disagreed with him.

Mix-up at the Plate

In a key play in the tenth inning of the third game of the 1975 World Series, Red Sox catcher Carlton Fisk bumped into the Reds' Ed Ambrister as he tried to field Ambrister's bunt. Fisk then threw wildly to second, trying to force Cesar Geronimo, who was on first. The wild throw put runners on second and third and Joe Morgan singled home Geronimo with the winning run, 6–5. Fisk argued that Ambrister interfered with him, but umpire Larry Barnett called it "a collision," not interference. The Reds went on to win the World Series. Did the umpire goof?

Branca's Burden

They are sad teammates — Brooklyn Dodger pitcher Ralph Branca (right) and coach Cookie Lavagetto. Minutes earlier, Branca had given up the historic home run to Bobby Thomson that enabled the New York Giants to upset the Dodgers in a 1951 National League playoff game. Announcer Russ Hodges' voice rose toward hysteria as he kept shouting over the radio: "The Giants win the pennant! The Giants win the pennant! The Giants win the pennant!" To this day, poor Branca still has to answer for that home-run pitch.

Hat Stuff

UPI

After winning his gold medal in the 20-kilometer walk at the Montreal Olympics in 1976, Mexico's Daniel Bautista proudly donned his sombrero.

The eternal comic, Bob Hope wore this bowler at a celebrity golf match in London. It didn't keep him from landing in the rough.

UPI

Beret and all, Frenchman Jean Boiteaux's father leaped into the water to embrace his son after Jean won the 400-meter freestyle gold medal in the 1952 Olympics at Helsinki, Finland.

When somebody scores three goals in hockey, it's called the hat trick. For scoring four goals in the 1983 National Hockey League All-Star Game, Wayne Gretzky was given this super sombrero.

Relief pitchers are known as firemen because they come to the rescue. The Elizabeth, New Jersey, Fire Department made Sparky Lyle an honorary member when he was with the Yankees, and Brooklyn's 13th Batallion made Dodger Hugh Casey honorary chief when he won a game in relief over the Yankees in the 1947 World Series.

Wrong-Way Riegels

Every year at Rose Bowl time the historians tell the tale of the most bizarre run ever recorded. It took place on January 1, 1929, when California played Georgia Tech. The center for California was a chunky, intelligent lad named Roy Riegels, who had a rare opportunity for a lineman to be a ball-carrier in the second quarter when a Georgia halfback fumbled on his own 35-yard line. Riegels (11) scooped up the ball, took a half dozen steps toward the Tech goal, then apparently having lost his sense of direction, he suddenly turned around and started toward his own goal, 65 yards away. His teammates began to realize what was happening and took off in desperate pursuit of him. By the time Riegels reached his own 20, his closest teammate was Benny Lom (28), who kept shouting, "Stop, you're going the wrong way." But Riegels was oblivious. Lom caught up with Riegels on the two-yard line and managed to slow him down. He was finally stopped two feet from the California goal. This led to a Tech safety and California lost the game, 8–7. The California center would be known forever as Wrong-Way Riegels.

Jerry Wachter

Spin Series

Usually it's the crashing linemen who give fits and spins to the quarterback, but in this instance the photographer, playing tricks with the camera, is the culprit as he captures quarterback Ken Anderson of the Cincinnati Bengals.

Tackle from the Bench

See No. 42 (black jersey) on the left along the sidelines in the upper left photo? He is fullback Tommy Lewis of Alabama. Running with the ball is Tommy Moegle of Rice. Lewis can't restrain himself and he races onto the field and tackles Moegle in the upper right photo. In the bottom photo, Lewis (far right) prepares to go back to the bench. Lewis' illegal tackle resulted in the referee awarding Rice a touchdown. Rice won the game, 28–6. It happened in the Cotton Bowl on January 2, 1954.

UPI

Forced Landing

It seemed a great day for football and ballooning. A Minnesota Viking fan decided to bring his hot-air balloon to New Orleans' Tulane Stadium for Super Bowl IV when the Vikings met the Kansas City Chiefs on January 11, 1970. In the pre-game festivities the fan and his balloon got out of control and landed in the stands, toppling a loudspeaker but otherwise doing no damage. The worst damage was done during the game: the Chiefs took the wind out of the Vikings' sails, 23-7.

Touchdown

The policeman isn't stopping traffic. He's signaling — even before the football official — that Tucker Frederickson of the New York Giants has scored a touchdown against the Buffalo Bills in a 1970 game at Shea Stadium.

UPI

UPI

A Shattering Experience

When Darryl Dawkins was with the Philadelphia 76ers, he proved that there were no shatterproof backboards. This slam dunk in Kansas City in 1979 caused a 50-minute delay in the game as Municipal Auditorium technicians installed a new backboard. Lawrence O'Brien, who was commissioner of the National Basketball Association, warned Dawkins afterwards that if he or any other player broke a backboard again, he would be ejected from the game.

Brief Encounter

It's no love affair and, remember, basketball is supposed to be a noncontact sport. The camera simply caught a rare midgame connection between Franklin College's Dan Masariu (22) and the University of Hawaii's Tom Zeimantz in a 1978 tournament game in Kansas City.

The Official Ball

Don (Slick) Watts was slick on the court with Seattle, New Orleans, and Houston; and his barber always made him look slick, too. So Slick inspired photographer Rich Pilling to create this photo with a ball head.

NBC-TV

Bursting the Bubble

Ballplayers and bubble gum are a team, and there are even bubble gum contests to see who blows the biggest bubble. Andy Messersmith, who pitched for more than a decade with the California and Los Angeles Angels, the Atlanta Braves, the New York Mets, and the Los Angeles Dodgers, bursts one here as Joe Garagiola looks on. George Brett of the Kansas City Royals also showed he could blow bubbles with the best of them in the Topps' Bazooka competition.

Topps

UPI

A Perfect Strike ══════════════

Illustrating that pitchers can sometimes be on the receiving end, Tom Seaver caught a fast one on the puss when he appeared in a "Kraft Music Hall" television show.

Fun and Games

The tiniest player ever to appear in a big-league game was 3-foot-7-inch Eddie Gaedel, who pinch-hit for the St. Louis Browns against the Detroit Tigers on August 19, 1951. It was a promotional stunt of St. Louis owner Bill Veeck and it had the desired effect: Eddie got a walk and a lot of publicity.

Al Schacht (left) and Nick Altrock, both of whom pitched in the majors, enjoyed later careers as baseball clowns. They're doing a tightrope-walking act here.

Max Patkin never made it to the big leagues as a player, but his antics gave him a permanent place in baseball as a comic in the minors and the majors.

Jay Johnstone, a big-league outfielder for a decade-and-a-half, liked to mask his feelings in the clubhouse.

Illegal Assist

It stands as the strangest finish ever in the Olympic marathon. It happened in London in 1908 in the 26-mile, 385-yard event that went from Windsor Castle to Shepherds Bush. As seen in the photo, Italy's Dorando Pietri, a pastry- and candy-maker, is in the final stages of the race. Seconds earlier, as he came reeling into the stadium, he'd fallen from exhaustion. The officials hauled Dorando back onto his jellied legs. He toppled several times, but finally staggered across the finish line. Behind him came Johnny Hayes, a New Yorker. At first Dorando was declared winner, but then he was disqualified because the officials had helped him. Hayes ended up with the gold medal.

Fallen Hopes

They were America's perfect pair as candidates for gold in the 1980 Winter Olympics at Lake Placid, New York. But Tai Babilonia and Randy Gardner lost their chance when Gardner fell and suffered a groin injury during the warmup for their performance. They were forced to withdraw from the competition.

On the Way to Greatness

Cassius Clay (who would become Muhammad Ali, heavyweight champion of the world) started boxing as a 12-year-old, 80-pounder in Louisville, Kentucky.

Pete Rose was the smallest player on his Cincinnati Knothole League team.

UPI

John F. Kennedy, the thirty-fifth President of the United States, was a fast runner, a quick passer, and perhaps the smartest little quarterback in the Greater Boston Private School League. He played for Dexter, a primary grade school in Brookline, Massachusetts.

23

UPI

The Long Count

Jack Dempsey has knocked down heavyweight champion Gene Tunney in the seventh round of their championship fight in 1927 before a crowd of 104,943 at Soldier Field, Chicago. Dempsey had been the champion and now he was trying to regain his title. It looked like the fight was over. But Dempsey failed to go to a neutral corner, as the rules demanded. And referee Dave Barry delayed the knockdown count. Five seconds ticked away before Barry started counting. By the count of nine — 14 seconds after he'd gone down — Tunney was back on his feet. And in the final three rounds he regained the lead he had in the early rounds. The referee and the judges awarded a unanimous decision to Tunney. If Dempsey had gone to the neutral corner immediately, he would have won by a knockout. And they never would have called it the "Long Count" bout.

Splashdown

Every golfer, from the best to the worst, has landed his ball in a water hazard. The golfer has the option of taking a penalty stroke and swinging anew on dry land or doing as William Nary did in this PGA tournament in St. Louis. He waded in after the ball and shot his way onto the fairway.

Dinner on Ice

Walter (Turk) Broda played goal for 16 seasons with the Toronto Maple Leafs and was so outstanding he landed in the Hockey Hall of Fame. A happy-go-lucky, roly-poly man, Turk was also a champion eater, as is suggested by this shot of him before a game.

Universal Pictures

"Slap Shot"

Paul Newman played peewee hockey as a boy in Cleveland, Ohio, but abandoned the sport when he joined a children's acting group at the age of 10. Forty years later, he laced on a pair of ice skates and became Reggie Dunlop, player-coach of the Charlestown Chiefs, in the movie *Slap Shot*. He called it the "toughest physical film I've ever done" (see Newman in the middle of the heap on ice). And after the shooting was over, Newman said, "I've really come to love this sport."

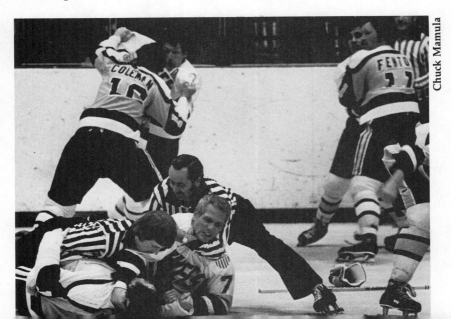

Chuck Mamula

Oops!

Clem McCarthy was the most famous of horse race announcers, but in 1947 he made the biggest blooper of his distinguished career. Broadcasting to a national radio audience, he announced that Faultless had won the Preakness Stakes when, in reality, the winner was Jet Pilot.

Sternoisms

Bill Stern was a celebrated radio announcer whose dramatic re-creations of sports happenings brought him a wide following. However, his accounts were often more fiction than fact, and sports experts dedicated to the truth labeled Stern's stories "Sternoisms."

29

The Superstars

All are superstars in their specialties, but they're testing themselves as competitors in "The Superstars," ABC-TV's annual spectacular. Baseball's Reggie Jackson is the weightlifter and, from the world of football, Dave Jennings bowls, Joe Theismann cycles, and Lynn Swann plays tennis.

Mile-a-Minute Murphy

Fortunately for Charlie Murphy, he didn't get a flat tire. On June 30, 1899, the 28-year-old Murphy pedaled a two-wheel racing bike over a measured mile at a speed better than 60 miles per hour. He achieved this feat on a specially-constructed board track laid between the rails of the Long Island Railroad on a level stretch near Hempstead, New York. "Mile-a-Minute Murphy," as he would be called from that instant on, was paced by a fast locomotive. He rode behind a coach fitted with a hood that served as a windbreaker.

UPI

Mud Battle

These soccer enthusiasts were not deterred by the swampy playing field in Burnham-on-Crouch, Essex, England. This was not the World Cup competition and they'd come to play. And that they did. Who won? It didn't matter.

UPI

The Babe Strikes Out

Babe Ruth is considered the greatest home run hitter of all time. It doesn't matter that Henry Aaron broke Ruth's career record of 714 homers or that Roger Maris, playing in more games, hit one more than Ruth's 60 for a single-season record. The Babe remains the greatest. He liked to play golf and bowl. But don't be misled by the boxing gloves he's wearing. In the early 1930s he decided to train in preparation for his "salary bout" with Colonel Jake Ruppert, then owner of the New York Yankees. Babe was making $80,000 a year. That was the highest salary in baseball in those days and a reporter asked Ruth if he thought it was right for him to be paid more than President Herbert Hoover, whose salary in 1931 was $75,000. "Why not?" Ruth replied. "I had a better year than he did!" As it turned out, the Babe did not win his fight with Ruppert. He signed a 1932 contract for $75,000, $5,000 less than his previous contract.

The Other Babe

As a track and field star, she won two gold medals and a silver in the 1932 Olympic Games. And she later became the world's greatest woman golfer. But Babe Didrikson's talents were displayed in many other sports as well. She could swim, dive, play tennis, bowl, play basketball and baseball. In the baseball photo, she's shown warming up at the spring training camp of the St. Louis Cardinals in 1931. No woman has ever played major-league baseball, but given the opportunity, with her ability and determination, the Babe could have done it.

Presentsidents at Play

UPI

Until he was injured, Ike Eisenhower was a promising halfback at West Point.

David Drew Zingg

John Kennedy loved sailing in the waters off Cape Cod.

Jimmy Carter swings away in a softball game against the press in Plains, Georgia.

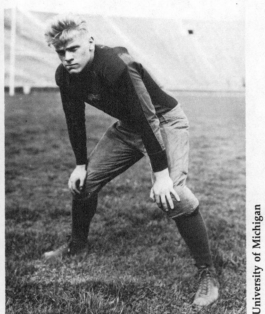

Gerry Ford was captain and center of the University of Michigan football team.

Harry Truman, a walker who always gave reporters a morning workout, presided over a calisthenics drill on the U.S.S. *Missouri*.

Historic Mask

If the Montreal Maroons' Clint Benedict hadn't permitted a shot that broke his nose, he might never have become the first hockey goalie to wear a mask. This was way back in 1930.

Faceless Pirate

After the Pittsburgh Pirates' Dave Parker suffered a broken cheek-bone in a 1978 collision with Mets' catcher John Stearns, he was out of action for a couple of weeks. He came back with a hockey mask that was enough to scare opposing pitchers.

UPI

Bird Fever

Mark (The Bird) Fidrych, a star pitcher for the Detroit Tigers in 1976, was introduced to "Big Bird" of Sesame Street before a game against the New York Yankees at Yankee Stadium.

Wide World

Phillie Phanatic

Philadelphia pitcher Tug McGraw took a ride on Phillie Phanatic, the team cheerleader, before the final game of the 1980 National League Championship Series against the Astros at Houston's Astrodome.

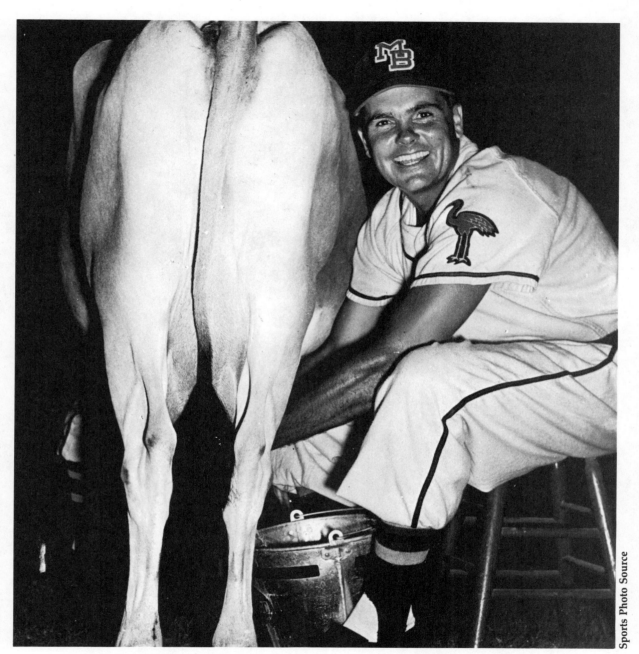

Side Show

Baseball promotions, especially in the minors, have featured every-
thing from footraces and fireworks to player participation in such
events as hitting baseballs into the stands, throwing a ball into a
barrel, heaving eggs at each other, and cow-milking contests.

On occasion, umpires have to clear dogs off the ballfield, but National League umpires Billy Williams (left) and Tom Gorman had a larger task before a 1974 Phillies-Braves game in Philadelphia. The elephant was part of a circus promotion and the umpires decided . . . if you can't lick 'em, join 'em.

Wide World

Look Out Below!

There is no hurdle in the Great Pardubice Steeplechase in Eastern Bohemia more difficult than this one. It is called the "Taxis Ditch" and, in this 1979 running of the event, only two riders were able to stay in the saddle after attempting the hurdle. It's no wonder that the riders rate this as the most challenging race on the European continent.

UPI

High Kick

Jimmy Pearsall was an always exciting, sometimes controversial outfielder who played for five different teams during his 17-year major-league career. For the first eight years he was with the Boston Red Sox and along the way he became the subject of a book, *Fear Strikes Out*, which later became a movie with Anthony Perkins playing Pearsall in the lead role. After Boston came Cleveland and it was with the Indians that he reached a career batting high of .322 in 1961, the year that he got into this scene in a game against the Yankees at Yankee Stadium. Two youngsters charged onto the field, interrupting the play and inspiring Pearsall to kick at one of them. The youngsters were arrested and the game resumed.

"Yer Out!"

Students at the Al Somers Umpire School in Florida learn the art of calling a man out.

Sports Photo Source

45

The Stormy World of Mighty Mac

He is one of the greatest tennis players of all time. He was only 20 when he won the U.S. Open Tennis Championship in 1979 and since then his triumphs at Wimbledon, in Davis Cup play and elsewhere, have thrilled fans around the globe. But John McEnroe, the brash left-hander from Douglaston, New York, has often been booed because of his antics — he pouts, he argues with officials, and displays bad manners in what is supposed to be a gentlemanly sport. There have been fines and point penalties, and the nickname "Super Brat" has followed him into manhood. But whenever he plays, watching him is an adventure — whether he's tumbling over the net, dropkicking his racquet or disputing an official's call.

UPI UPI

UPI

Battle of the Sexes

Bobby Riggs, who had won the Wimbledon and U.S. Championships
in 1939, liked to say that the best of the female tennis pros couldn't
even beat him, "an old man with one foot in the grave." So this
55-year-old challenged 29-year-old Billie Jean King to a match at
Houston's Astrodome on September 20, 1973. Billie Jean, a fireman's
daughter from Long Beach, California, who has won the most
Wimbledon crowns in history, was a crusader in building the female
professional game. The match was witnessed by a crowd of 30,472,
the largest ever in tennis, and more than 50 million others watched
on prime-time television. King shut up Riggs, the outspoken hustler,
by winning, 6-4, 6-3, 6-3. She collected $100,000 in this winner-
take-all event.

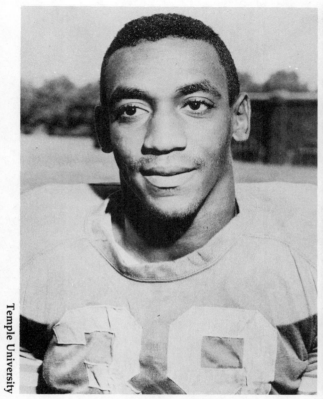

No Comic on the Playing Field

He was a serious football player — basketball, too — at Temple University in Philadelphia and, after he became a successful comedian, Bill Cosby wielded a tennis racquet in celebrity competitions.

Good Morning, David

"As soon as the snow melted and there were patches of brown grass showing through, soggy and wet, I remember thinking, 'It's okay to get my glove and go out and begin playing baseball.'" So said David Hartman, the host of ABC-TV's *Good Morning, America.* Hartman is a bona fide ballplayer, as he proved in his days at Mt. Hermon Prep in Massachusetts, where he captained the team and was a catcher and first baseman. Later, at Duke, he broadcast the university's baseball games. After graduation, Hartman played baseball in the Air Force, but he chose acting for his career. On the West Coast, once he'd achieved status in the title role in the *Lucas Tanner* television series, in which he was a former St. Louis Cardinal pitcher who became a high-school teacher, Hartman got to be friendly with the Los Angeles Dodgers, and later the San Francisco Giants. He likes to schedule trips to spring training, where he lives every boy's fantasy by putting on the uniform of a major-league team and taking his cuts at the plate.

American Airlines

Yogi to the Fore ══════════

As manager of the New York Yankees, Yogi Berra doesn't have much time off. But occasionally he gets in a round of golf and no matter how he shoots, Yankee owner George Steinbrenner can't second-guess him. Of course, Yogi is less known as a golfer than as the man whose funny comments have made the sports world chuckle. Consider . . . "We made too many wrong mistakes." . . . "You observe a lot by watching." . . . "Nobody goes there anymore. It's too crowded."

51

Packey East

There once was a young boxer in Cleveland, Ohio, who fought under the name of Packey East. He gave up the sport in favor of a career as a comedian. His name: Bob Hope. He's shown here squaring off for fun in 1951 against former heavyweight champion Jack Dempsey and in 1968 at the opening ceremonies of the new Madison Square Garden, where he had a mock bout with former heavyweight champion Rocky Marciano. The referee was singer/actor Bing Crosby.

UPI

Surprise for the Champ

Leon Spinks had won the Olympic light heavyweight title in Montreal in 1976. He had been a professional for only a year and a half when he stepped into the ring against heavyweight champion Muhammad Ali on February 15, 1978, in Las Vegas, Nevada. He was 24, 12 years younger than Ali, who had lost only twice in 57 bouts as a professional. Ali was a heavy favorite, but this was not to be his night. Spinks drew blood in the fourth round and got stronger as the fight continued. And it was apparent, when they began the fifteenth and final round, that Ali would need a knockout, or at least a knockdown, to keep his crown. He got neither. Spinks was awarded the decision. "He may be the greatest, but I'm the latest," Spinks proudly proclaimed. Exactly six months later, in a return engagement in New Orleans, Ali decisioned Spinks to win the crown for the third time.

"The Rifleman"

His greatest fame would come when he went to Hollywood and
became an actor in films and on television. Viewers knew him for
his title role in *The Rifleman*, but Chuck Connors was a star long
before he went before the cameras. At Brooklyn's Adelphi Academy
he played many sports — he's the lanky, blond lad heaving the
shot and running — and he later played basketball for the Boston
Celtics and first base for the Brooklyn Dodgers (one game) and the
Chicago Cubs (66 games).

UPI The Connors Collection

Jon Simon

"The Natural"

Yes, it is Robert Redford. He's in the role of a 35-year-old slugger playing for the New York Knights in the 1984 film, *The Natural*. Redford bats and throws left-handed and is, indeed, a natural athlete. Joe Castellano, a semipro player who had a bit part in the movie, said of Redford: "He has a good, short stroke at bat and throws with the fluid motion of a ballplayer. It was obvious to all of us that he was no stranger to a ballfield."

The Sporting Matthau

Walter Matthau (center) is at home in the sporting world as a fan and in some of his acting roles. He was a sportswriter in *The Odd Couple* and a manager in *The Bad News Bears*. And over the years he has played in exhibition games against the media at Dodger Stadium. In this 1975 photo, he's flanked by comedian Jerry Lewis (right) and Steve Garvey, then a Dodger. Garvey gave Matthau a few pointers, but his "Stars" were beaten this time by a collection of sportswriters and TV commentators.

UPI

On the Way to the White House

Ronald (Dutch) Reagan was a 120-pound tackle on the undefeated Dixon (Illinois) High School football team in 1926. He switched to guard at Eureka College and, although not a star, "he gave 150 percent," one of his teammates said. After graduation he became a sports announcer before he headed West for an acting career in Hollywood films. There, one of his roles was as George (Gipper) Gipp of Notre Dame (pictured above) in *Knute Rockne — All-American.*

A Saturday Hero

Nobody had to show Burt Reynolds how to hold a football. He was a star at Florida State before he became an actor. His college experience was helpful when he appeared in the movie *The Longest Yard*. He's shown with Ray Nitschke, the former Green Bay Packer linebacker. Shot at a Georgia penitentiary, the film contains lengthy and realistic action football sequences. The highlight of the movie is a football game played between a team of prison guards, led by Nitschke, and a team of prisoners led by Reynolds. "Burt is a fine athlete," Nitschke said. "He's a man's man, a very physical, tough guy. There were times when his stand-in was supposed to get hit by me and he would flinch or shy away. Burt would step in and say, 'I'll do it.' "

Garden Variety

It has been called the world's most versatile stage. For more than 100 years, New York's Madison Square Garden (on four sites) has been the scene of an unmatched variety of sport and spectacle. From circuses to political conventions, from basketball and hockey games to track meets, from championship fights to rock-and-roll performances, Garden events have even included, as the photos indicate, ski-jumping, a six-day bike race, and public swimming.

60

UPI

Gnats to You

In this rare scene at a game in Chicago, play had to be halted when an army of insects descended on Hoyt Wilhelm, who was pitching for the Baltimore Orioles against the White Sox. Wilhelm (15) watched as coach Al Vincent waved a towel. It had no effect. Then the umpires and a batboy tried spraying insecticide. After that, the groundskeepers burned paper and sprayed some more. Finally a smoke bomb was used and the insects took off for points unknown. Wilhelm survived the attack and won the game. It took place in 1959.

Roll Out the Barrel

The sport of leaping over barrels on ice skates, born in Holland centuries ago, has long been a staple at Grossinger's, the Catskill Mountain resort in New York State. Barrel jumping was introduced there in 1951 by former Olympic speed-skating champion Irv Jaffee and it evolved into championship competition that has been telecast on the national networks.

Circling the Globetrotters

They are athletes and they are comedians, and for more than 50
years they have taken the game of basketball around the world.
They have played in drained swimming pools, on dance floors and
Navy flight decks, in opera houses and bull rings, and with their
antics, including a warm-up routine to the finger-snapping tune of
"Sweet Georgia Brown," they have delighted fans everywhere.